ANOTHER WAY

'What is the shape of a lost country? What fills that shape,
like water? Cross a body of water towards home. No, away
from home. It's not possible, mid-image, pre-scene, to say
which direction this water is flowing towards. In Alycia
Pirmohamed's *Another Way to Split Water*, a reader gets to taste
arrival before arrival, a form of tenderness that refracts: "an
inherited vanishing/through the slit of a dream." Or: "Inward"
+ "burgeon" = "loving what I can"? These are the questions the
book emanates, perhaps, each time it's opened in
a café, or on a plane.'
BHANU KAPIL

'Alycia Pirmohamed's astute and moving poems dwell in a
longing that's a "pattern embossed" on the skin. She transfigures
yearning into intimacies with family, Canadian prairies, and
rain that "knows how to fall in Gujarati". An intimacy with
language is evident on each page: sonic-rich phrasing, imagery
that leaps and soars, and an astonishing attentiveness to the line.
Pirmohamed is an immensely gifted poet. Her first book
is an opening, a marvel.'
EDUARDO C. CORRAL

'Alycia Pirmohamed's debut, *Another Way to Split Water*, is an electric, taut, and glimmering achievement: the poet conjures with clarity and intelligence a world that is marked by longing, loss, and lost lands. She splits and gathers water like hair, elegizing and praising relationships to mothers, lovers, and God, but ultimately, this is a love song to and a lament of the self, estranged and beautiful. Here is an incredible new voice, allowing us to listen to her tender song.'

ARIA ABER

'This is how *Another Way to Split Water* moves, wending through ossuaries and great plains, making oxbow lakes of prayers and their origins, bifurcating desire and discovery till each word holds its own river. You will want to map the navigations of these poems. You will be compelled to orbit their magnetic and inimitable oscillations. Ravenous, I reach for the depths Pirmohamed has herein abseiled.'

SHIVANEE RAMLOCHAN

ANOTHER WAY TO SPLIT WATER

Alycia Pirmohamed

First published in Great Britain in 2022 by
Polygon, an imprint of Birlinn Ltd.

Birlinn Ltd
West Newington House
10 Newington Road
Edinburgh EH9 1QS

9 8 7 6 5 4 3 2 1

www.polygonbooks.co.uk

ISBN 978 1 84697 603 2
EBOOK ISBN 978 1 78885 528 0

British Library Cataloguing-in-Publication Data
A catalogue record for this book is available
from the British Library.

The publisher gratefully acknowledges investment from
Creative Scotland towards the publication of this book.

Typeset in Verdigris MVB by Polygon, Edinburgh
Printed and bound by CPI Group (UK) Ltd, Croydon CR0 4YY

To Timothy

CONTENTS

PART I

PART II

PART I

The sea separates us, separates me from getting to know the
ephemeral thing that pushes another ephemeral thing to go on.

                              – Vi Khi Nao

forgive me   i cannot teach you to say my name   i am from
anywhere halved by water

                              – Safia Elhillo

FADED

Say the word dark
translates to how I fold my body

like a fig
against a stippled moon.

Pull a string of sorrows from
my mouth.

Remind me that I am not a swan –

I am a long night of rain
with my mother's eyes.

Hold my tasbih to my heart.

Imagine we are
elk walking into tall grass.

This dream is the sky opening,

this dream is a river of faces.

This dream is all of the pine trees
replaced with smoke.

I call out to the water and the wind
scatters my thoughts,

fashions distances within me.

I call out *Allah* –

if I look up, I see a ghost
in the canopy.

MEDITATION WHILE PLAITING MY HAIR

I part my hair straight down the middle,
a river on either side –
in the past, someone shaped like me
poured water from a metal carafe
straight into my mouth,
the echo of my river submerged in your river –
lately, I read about storms all night
because there is no lightning here; instead
I see the wind pull down the tautness
of trees and the swans at the lagoon part
through the wreckage.
Each one is another translation for love
if love was more vessel than loose thread.

        Once, we sat poolside outdoors in Dar es Salaam
        and I chose survival over your body.
        Why is it I only ever see the night heron alone?
        I braid neatly together my hair, soaked by salt
        and the moss of a body I do not touch,
        the spine of a book left open on the page
        I forgot to bookmark,
        the spine of a book I left out in a storm,
        each of its rooms sliding into our margins,
        into all these tendrils of blank space – tell me, when
           did I let us splinter?

There were some tones of night
I could not bear,

that I could not gather in my arms
to hold onto.

Small town nights.
Cigarette nights, plumage swelling and drifting

into a concaved sky.
Nights where I harnessed myself

to the canola fields, alfalfa
leaves, elk sightings

unelegiacally, with no magnitude of loss,
no understanding of letting go.

That was fourteen years ago, and now
the echo is half-dream

made of skimmed milk and cane sugar stars.
The other half?

Radio static, the white noise of prairies
twenty minutes outside of the city

where, for miles,
all you will ever see is that one spotted calf

walking into the sunset.
Smaller nights, smaller even

than the needle of a broken compass
flickering back and forth,

then hovering briefly as if to say –
you have reached your destination,

or, perhaps, *you are not lost.*
Then pointed toward the glimpse of spruce

trees outside my bedroom window
holding close all of the stray cats underneath

as each stammer of lightning
flinched across.

Those are the nights that dial,
that leave a message then hang up, hang you up

under the moon,
into a storm, into solitude.

I WANT THE KIND OF PERMANENCE IN A BIRDWATCHER'S CATALOGUE

At Lochend Park, swans tendril together
the shape of my longing,

a languid rippling trail of water.
I lean over the edge of the pond, see petals of my face

glinting in the water, a Tuesday morning vase
of unhurried thoughts and magenta

lipstick –

Any birdwatcher will tell you
that winged boats

do not howl through their sharp, pyramid beaks.

That sound clicking through
waterlogged bodies

must be the prosody of my own desires.
I shower in the summer solstice light

and read my morning prayers off the cracked
screen of my phone

– Forgi/ve me

as if a corner of my yearning refracts into an alternate
universe,

a parallel world, a symmetrical ruffled wing.

I reorient myself on the path, into a body turned
away from its doubling,

sick of my own gaze staring back.

There is departure in every window, in every
wind-rustled seed.

 – Forgi/ve me
for desiring the permanence of a birdwatcher's catalogue

each line of pigment an absolute, a trail of ink
never slipping beyond its typeset world.

HINGE

Tonight I am all joint and animal dark. My heel blots out the moon,
    vanishes the small nod of light. And yes,
I prayed today, verging into my bismillah before settling
        on the broken.

I stoop into my longings, plot a seed in every corner. Last week
    I titled another page with my body
        and surrendered every bending, splitting line of myself
to the making.

When we refer to plants, we call this positive phototropism,
        a body rivering toward the light.
I want to river toward the light. I want to lean my neck toward
    a thing until I, too, become ism,

scientific and named into truth.
    Today, I walked through a dream that wasn't mine, and I
        thought of you waiting at the end of it,
as if to gather me

and maybe that's just the kind of woman I am – no matter
    how many times I halve the moon or find myself in a room
without a window, I know Allah
        sees everything, every hand planting something new,

every metaphor for the tree it becomes. And *yes*,
    I prayed today, but planting my palms together has never
        felt like blossoming up the side of a mountain.
The only time these hands have ever flowered,

have ever been used for something good,
    was that spring at Yamnuska, where we found a clear
blue door of glacial water, and I walked right through
    your reflection.

THE FISH THAT HALVED WATER

Dusk meets water meets the history of my eye.
I walk into the water –

I walk into the shimmering body of a fish as the river's rinse
and monsoon knot my memory.

It is already night and all I have learned is the past
is a version of this earth

where few things have a name.
I glide my way through the anonymity of ghosts.

This is the landmark of ruins I have become: a woman
following every weaving *hush*,

every tendril of water in search of a true story.
Listen, I expected the Atlantic to show me

all that ruptured when woman after woman after locust
crossed an ocean.

There are too many names for canyon and every day
I hold those distances in my mouth –

all the kilometres my longing has travelled.
In the middle of the night, I walk right into my dreams

and cluster with the other lost sisters of the moon,
our bodies blushing out from the forest's velour.

In the middle of the night, I walk right into a dream
where the grass pickerel scissor through

my every plot of land. The thing about being halved
is all the loose ends will sneak up on you

whether you're slicing zambarau or dragging a toboggan
up a hill, threading in and out of the evergreens

as you climb. There are too many ways to say cleave,
but one day I'll split into myth

and pass through the mouths of a hundred generations.
I am woman after woman after spooling

woman, ensorcelled by water that twins and fissures
and halves into worlds.

AFTER THE HOUSE OF WISDOM

Once, there was a version of this river
overwhelmed with first translations.
A river shaped like the philosopher's memory.
Origins are also small memories
and there is an ethics to remembering –
I hear lilting from below the evening green
that houses our episodic ghosts.
Why is it that water edges into every
paragraph – every lexical formation?
Perhaps it is the other way around, small
rivers uncoiling into ink on this version
of my eyes. So, I rinse in a bath of citations,
feeling as human as the rest of them,
unfolding my spine in one long extended verse.
Yes, like I am someone's past, spilling out rust
onto palms, reading the wounds of the land –
like I am pouring out into a dream,
into a basin of dark peaks, into another's
history. Yes, I desire knowledge,
whether physical or moral or spiritual.
This kind of longing is a pattern embossed
on my skin. And each of my faces remember
their very first reflection ::
I am doubled. This language doubles me.

WHEN THE WOLVES APPEAR

When the wolves appear, I know I am dreaming.
Give me back my dark.   They call out in Gujarati & no howling
could terrify me as much.   The wolf-eyes look like eyes in family
photographs. They follow me.   I run & don't look back.
I am terrified of the land.   In the sea, my body is a vase
filled with ovate black stones.
I sink   I sink   I sink.   Where have the wolves gone & where is
the voice that held the whorls of my fingers in its clay?
Is it fair to wish for them now?
They don't belong in this version of a version
of India that wets my hair & deposits my skin onto the shore—
to get to the bone.   To get to the language.
I want to say *yes*   I want to become a stream of sugar cane & milk
& wash through the aquifers.   To pick up slim stalks
of clove along the way.   I want to carry my dark with me.
Stretch out legs of jasmine vine & call out
to the deep space between the moons.   Every night I open my mouth.
Every night my mouth is an orbiting elliptical *no*.

NERIUM OLEANDER

When she opens
her body

there is glistening
oleander.

How much of her skin
is a body of water?

Nerium
because she is a flood

of rain as it falls
into a river,

because she sprouts
in rich alluvials.

She is allowing
herself

to love herself,
every invisible space

and darkness.
She is learning how

not every root
traces back

to a name. *Olea*
meaning

somewhere, she has lost
her origin,

meaning
she will follow the stream

and come into
glaucous bloom.

SELF-ADDRESSED

Into the tall dusk,
into the tamarack wood,
into a city which at this hour
could be the shape
of any migrating bird.

This is me, driving straight
into my own life,
past the river frozen over
slick, the chokecherry's saw
toothed edges –

into the roughage
of memories that surface slow
and tired, memories like
the stars enacting
what is already gone.

I am grasping at
the things easiest to love:
Anas acuta, *Pinus resinosa*,
Anthaxia inornata, the language
of the prairies,

syntax that I have held
like a dog with birch in her
mouth, a landscape that runs
through a body,
is a body –

into the boiling ginger,
into the neck of a loved one
folded like a leveret,
folded like a letter closing with
I wish you were here,

I wish you were here –

PRAIRIE STORM

We shoo away the hornet
as she lands on a grain of saffron rice.

Outside, the sky sparks like a wet nerve.
It must be lonely to be a storm,

long stems of water scattering sidelong
in a suddenly vacant wide.

The rain knows how to fall in Gujarati.
Afterward, bellies full

of clove heads and yolk, we spill
into the yard and read in dark rivers.

How quickly the landscape mothers
those stray tears,

bushels of mustard anchoring the roots
of an indivisible language.

And we marvel at how something
carried such a long distance

can fill the prairies like a vase, as we,
ourselves, pour and pour.

WHEN THE STORM ENDS

When the storm ends, the city looks as though it is
an elongated band of ice

as though it is 2007 again – when late afternoon tugged
away the lilacs and all that remained was Banff

in winter: green-leaf tea and lukewarm lamentation.
God never touched anything here,

not in this memory, haunted by the cacophony of grey
partridges and cicadas all evening

and you at the driveway, a little terrier by your heels.
Back then, I wrote about the wind chimes bellowing their last

call before the snow turned us impressionistic,
and about your howling, resounding like the full moon.

It all sinks away – partridges   cicadas   your skin   my own . . .
The city is back, white foam receding into the horizon.

In its wake, it uncovers every imprint: us in Florence,
Oregon, on the Pacific coast

where we laughed at oysters and how alien
they looked gathered and gleaming on wet rocks.

On the same coast, the waves pulled back the sand,
wiping it clean as if nothing had ever occurred –

I think of writing you a letter, something soothed
by the address: *dear*, with Virginia on the stamp

though I have never been there. I'd account for
all the sounds of my memory –

how loudly they echo, how they hurl themselves at me
like the threads of a storm.

I AM LEARNING THROUGH MOUTHS

My mouth is a pink shadow, the penumbra
of lightning over repetitions of mountain and white spruce.
It sips at Barrier Lake. I have so many photographs of that lake –
in one my heart unspools like the language of my prayers.
Site of drool and hunger, my mouth withholds a waterlogged
bismillah

> next to my tongue. My tongue is sometimes bright red.
> It dives into the archipelagos of a fruit called miracle.
> I catch the seeds of all my devotion. I think *is this not why*
> *Allah gave me teeth?* To gnaw at sweet words and hear the wind
> scatter.

> > I recite du'a only to renarrativise it again.
> > Who was it that told me not to trust my memory?
> > That looking back is like unfolding into deep space.
> > – my first photograph of an elk as it leaps across the
> > plains and my mouth opens in witness. I think
> > *God*

for this
I still love you.

LAPSE

How I know I have returned from dreaming:
if I reach out, I will touch oranges.

I prefer ghosts.
Not oranges, but the mouth,

the burned hibiscus-stained lips.
In the memory, you have a short haircut.

You open your mouth to reveal a cluster of roses.
How I know the truth has been replaced –

the roses you pin to my chest
are more accurate than the oranges.

They peel off your tongue. Petals for words.
Veritas – every secret let go.

Luxury is not the fruit itself. It is a trillion
buds frothing your skin

allowing you to disrobe into morning light.
It is your presence, stepping beyond

the past tense and into this room,
into a moment of clean and seamless figuration.

LOVE POEM WITH ELK AND PUNCTUATION

To taste water
on the surface of a mirror –

to love, even briefly, the elk of your own tongue.

We become a myth that will cleave in the middle.

I admire spooling lotus after lotus after.
Fragment of my body:

brown edges, the whorl of a question mark
and you? Night's quiet whisper.

We become a bridge that crosses the chasm.

It takes a moon or two, a slivering, to chapter.
I look at the fringe

and watch evening kick her feet right through.

We, too, become hoofs of light and feel our way
around tenderness –

this is a dream and we are the ruminants in it.

I want to know the ellipsoidal of you.
How you move

from polygon to speckle, rectangle to unravel.

In the water, I stretch out until I am lagoon
and you are the coral

reef at my toes,
until I am the lotus that blossoms after!

HAWWA DISCOVERS ADAM BY THE RIVER

She is bird,
she is every vertebra

that bends, twists, cracks

and comes undone. Near the river, there is a man
naked and shivering.

Hawwa extends her spine,
uplifts

her long neck, glides her body like a boat across
land

engorged with dew and apple blossom.

She is root, water, earth,
and every

whisper of wind. Imagine her eyes,

imagine the rattle of her heart,
or imagine the sting

of hot sand on her bareness, all of it born from the same
seed

and heartache. Hawwa carries the dusk
on her back,

eats long grains of saffron rice, pleasures in the half-light
of a crescent moon.

Hawwa does not ask
how this man came to be,

only sets him down among the wildflowers,

his body a sieve,
oxlip slipping through.

HAWWA IS CREATING HER GARDEN

Before her, the clay
of evergreen and juniper and oak.

Hawwa drinks sweet water from the well,

studies the spine of each tree,
kisses each face

she finds in the river.

Hawwa is this garden. Look closely

at the tasbih beads that glisten
like blackberries

on the bough.

Hawwa is olivine
and zinc,

she has planted seeds beneath the highest point
of the sun

and unfolded her body
onto the earth. She rises

like an eagle
and laughs like a wasp.

Hawwa loves many things and what she loves

she gives a name – the birds
that *ki ki ki*

are northern flickers. She cracks open a
pistachio

and delights in its snap.

Hawwa is heart and animal and breast and god.

ENDEARMENTS

I have itemised
your oak leaf long limb wild

& have begun to name you things like
'summer eclipse

in my offline calendar' or even 'sleeping
under the stars

in a Walmart parking lot'
& honestly

that kind of romance is okay with me
because secretly I have also named you 'river of pine'

& 'blossoming spring flower along the path to
Mount Yamnuska'.

There is also your skin & my skin,
there is also the way skin & skin are two

vastly different things
that this language has difficulty

capturing:
'every constellated mole' &

'pillar of dark shade'.
How all of these names describe the way

we coexist
& exist within one another –

the way you disappear into the trees
& I follow.

YOU KNOW IT BUT IT DON'T KNOW YOU
after Tako Taal's artwork by the same name

1.

she places the silverware
one thumb slip   beyond the edge

beyond the pattern that repeats and repeats –

beyond the sun
coloured spade

beyond the petiole   's slant that repeats

into / the next world.

11.

[Baduja]   [   ]

Even with the backs of wild rowan
    behind her.

Even when the wind calls out a
    different name.

Even with smoke ebbing from every
    mistranslation.

Even as the tree splits neatly into its
    metaphors.

Even though they only meet at the
    centrefold of a photograph.

Even as the metaphor splits into its
    likened parts.

Even though a landscape can change a
    body.

Even with the inherited memory of
    water between past and present.

Even though her body is riven with
    departures.

Even when the deer bounds across a
    grove toward the next in line.

~~Because this is a version of a version~~
    ~~of rainfall.~~

~~Because she is told they mirror the~~
    ~~same face.~~

~~Because they do not meet beyond a~~
    ~~border of glass.~~

~~Because a tongue splits through a~~
    ~~throng of trees.~~

~~Because his image is made truer by the~~
    ~~fabric of her dreams.~~

~~Because the two of them are likened~~
    ~~parts.~~

~~Because she plots a seed in every~~
    ~~conditional space.~~

~~Because she crosses water and because~~
    ~~water is the tether back.~~

~~Because she follows herself until she~~
    ~~is tender.~~

~~Because time gathers behind her like a~~
    ~~V of birds.~~

III.

    :: Notice how maroon is a colour that deepens
    with every pour

    :: Formerly a constellation of spring in her palm

    :: See also: the hand that swept along a spine
    of berries x years ago

    :: The past streams from a pitcher like thirst
    into the present tense

    :: She is made in his image therefore she is
    counter-memory

    :: See also: inherited memory of [er's fa e]

    :: Today the maroon skin of her fingertip
    is an imprint of yesterday's pour

    :: She is made in his image therefore she is
    a sieve

    :: Inevitably the future sifts through

:: Sieve is another word for counter-memory

:: In both cases the daughter fills in what
   remembrance leaves out

:: Liquid decants from the metal carafe until
   the bowl is full

Inheritance is the possession of second sight ::

IV.

This body

                unravels

its

                cacophony

        across

        time

                country

wound   the great sea.

This body is a body of water is the unsaid page. It unravels its invisible sheaves. A flood of light glistens into a cacophony of sea birds. I look through the viewfinder with my dominant eye. I look across the endless water. Sometimes my eye is a stanza with only one long line attempting to reach you. When does a country become a window? All morning I am a metonymic slide. This body reaches only as far as it needs to. There is no irrigating a wound if that wound is the great sea.

MIDNIGHT VESSEL ACROSS THE GREAT SEA

What kind of river, then, has no middle?
                                    – Édouard Glissant

Another bloom after the first bloom   inheritance is a form
of second sight   in the past someone with my birthmarks
predicted the next moon   the upheaval   my own ebb.
My body is the echo of her iambs   a tradition that sieves
right through   my ancestor's thread.   I am slick with
rosewater and cat's eye   – I can't choose between
survival or pleasure.   In the past   someone who looked
like me fell   into the valley of roses   five times a day.
This echo is   another velvet petal   submerged in the drool
of my mouth   I am submerged   in the drool of her mouth.
My second sight is an heirloom   a volume of sonnets
passed down   a line of flight   as if she is more image
than intent   more midnight than syllable   the eye before
the eye   the root beneath my poem.   I am a remembrance
and she is my volta –   an echo blooms   this echo is her hair
parting into my hair   she is the fine dark strand   across
my memory   she glides like a reed   a silhouette of green
across the great sea   her poetry strikes through   my window
like a stone   breaking the skin   memory of water.

PART II

Our time is recursive and forking. Our time is a garden in which all realities are simultaneously possible.

– Sun Yung Shin

The heart cannot fill with occasion, the full particulars of a narrative I don't remember.

– Nisha Ramayya

WELCOME

You know better than to feel welcome at anything resembling a border –
at least you do now anyway, as you reckon anew with the boreal ahead,

dark cone after dark cone, a hem of blue light signalling the horizon
as it peeks through the geometries.

This drive will always remind you of childhood's pitch-black nightfall
and all those headlights in lieu of moons.

Here you'd watch the glow in front of you, settled on one side of that other
border, that other hem, rivering between young girl and womanhood.

*

It is the drive you remember most –
Vilna, Alberta is half buck and half headlight in the memory

of one body separating from another, the split
into *them* and *us* once the towers fell.

And everything you have written since that moment
cut open every wound you didn't know you had

is haunted by extra spaces in your lineation,
your every impulse to add another gap,

another leap into some self you'll never recall.
Them and *us* coincided with rural thunderstorms, with searching

for a stray tabby beneath the stammering pine,
a cat which, earlier, your classmate had jabbed and kicked

in a violence you will never understand. Welcome
edges further and further away

even as you walk right into your childhood eyes.
This is how swiftly a country will turn its dial away from you.

Even as a young girl, you found fragments
of the broken mirror that same country handed you

in which you saw not your own reflection
but something jagged, something too dark, too dark, too dark.

*

You know this is where you curve east toward Redwater,
and if the sun were out, there would be cattle alongside the road,

calves on their rickety legs, whole herds of glittering eyes behind the fences.
And on the other side? Birch:

So much of it that you'd think in this case, a group of trees must
also be called a herd, with their own rickety young stirring in the wind.

All of this you imagine as you glance out the rear-view mirror
and somehow you know this road is the line between it all –

what is named or what is nameless
what is memory or what is seed.

Look at this new version of yourself. A self-portrait so precise in its
languages that at times she lives only in the penumbra of your words:

the young girl who counted out her bismillahs in the schoolyard
each time lightning embossed the field.

There is also that day long before they fell,
when you mixed egg yolks in a friend's kitchen after a slow walk

from one trough to another in the rain.
Surely there was peace then, an innate sort of harmony –

the kind you imagine must bring a cow to water.
The highway treads north, Vilna now printed neatly on the road signs

and you can no longer tell if you are heading forward or backward
save for the numbers ticking down.

ELSEWHERE

She did not know the shape of
this country –   wide   darkjagged

bend in the river, rock elm withering,
everything withering

into unfamiliar, needled forest.
She was searching for the water and the water

was a heartache tongued by wild deer.

In northern Alberta, she was a line of crow
edging into the unknown,

a woman caught between fennels of a dream
and long mouths of birch.

Even the key of her body –
      jaggedlong   gentledark –

could not unlock this landscape.

Sometimes there is a fog thick enough
to hide the trees

and she imagines this country unwithers,
becomes a different land,

where her body is shaped like the river
and the river

is shaped like belonging.

ORIGIN OF WATER II

as a child   she wore a skirt of seagulls
and was afraid of the dark   called her mother god
because what else

could mother an ocean but god?   she ate nankhatai
and plaited her hair   she smelled of cardamom

newly crushed and boiled   she split into spring's tulips,
carried a jar of condolences   just in case.

she was a daughter caught praying in the mountains.

she was stone through stone   melodic   a vase of trees
rattled by her name: water, like the roots that hold the earth
together.

ginan and its woven stanzas.   she is the sound of a
messenger calling for another bird   another

metaphor for god.   as a child   how was she to know
what to call beloved?

PERSEPHONE'S CROSSINGS

I.

I am born into this story of selves,
one that leaves the fruit to rust,

the other that cuts the sweet –

this memory

is shadow
is bruise
is coyote – *I wish*

I never knew the sound of howling.

In this version, I am more or less already
gone,

a daguerreotype under a long exposure.

In this version, the nectarines are ripe:
copacetic   falling off the tree   sweet

ready

& I am a woman, not girl.

Woman with mother's eyes,
woman with a maroon mouth –

woman with distances already within me.

11.

Dear Mother,

Forgive me for this disappearing act. Sorrow begets
sorrow & I know

why the clove blossoms no longer flower.

Call it what you will – violence, abduction,
a kidnapping by wolves –

that morning, the earth split apart like a mouth
reciting du'a

& there I was

some foundling taken into its arms,
diving into the archipelagos,

a scattering homeland.

Mother, I still long for our maine coon cat
& grandfather's old records,

for my kitten heels
& tamarind paste & fresh cilantro,

for your evening hair
& sundown languages,

every third prayer,
every bismillah that does not live here,

in this heart beneath the heart.

Sometimes I mistake faces in the halite –
there is only smoke,

the assimilation of a lost country,
where every cold season is now a refrain

of your sorrow.

I keep apologising.

III.

If you ask what I remember
beyond this story,

I will say 'terrifying
black hole'

& nothing else.

How can I describe this country whose
features rotate

in opposite directions

pulling apart the clay, pith
& horsehair stitched into the earth.

'plurality,

heartache, cruel magician –'

a storm?

Here is my palm. Here are the seeds.

This is my last
mercurial surrender –

because I know how a landscape
can break a body

into its fragments.

I know that I, too, have become
the fruit

bearing too many histories within.

The seeds glisten.

You have asked,
so listen: I will never be whole.

IV.

Soon the body will forget itself
& become another dream

of the same longing.

At last, unroofed,
I travel vertical, charge into a motherland

riven with arrivals.

Remind me how figs taste
on the side of a mountain,

how grain springs into gold,

& how cranes in the sky own everything
at once.

Take me away from this hive, this
bitten nail.

Alight my eyes with kohl & read me epistles.

In the bright sun, everything
is stippled –

perhaps this is the edge of waking,
when the body feels like oil over water,

or sleek like nettles after a long rain.

Forgive me,
the arils were so sweet

& the birds so much like home.

SELF-PORTRAIT WITH FISH EYES

I am a woman who is longdark
language

a woman who eats fish eyes
to feel close to mother

a woman who loves whole milk
whole figs and single dimensions

I am a woman with *this* many faces
this being not a number

but a rhizome of turmeric
eyelashes sweeping

against the smoke
a lily's open mouth

my voice   such tall spruce

I am a woman that carried
my first heartache

before I was born
a woman whose irises are

split open seams
spilling a longdark bloodline –

MY BODY IS A FOREST

There is a face in the trees.

I lost a language
           to the gap-toothed   birch.

Even the pine has learned how to swoon
when the wind
           deposits a secret.

A country is born knowing what it means
to waver.

A lost country is made by its daughters

and shame begins as a seed
           that blossoms perennially

      throughout generations.

Clove keeps the cha bitter – for every dark
cross

I apologise

      because I could not read the recipe
written in my grandmother's neat script.

I added cinnamon   crushed anise   mountain
slope

    and too many quartered
Canadas –

once I watched a mule deer unfold her limbs
and vanish

      among the haloed trees

fog uncoiling at her heels   a ghost
inviting her

into its loosened borders.

In the blood of every migrant
    there is a map pointing home   this body

is an ode to the scattered landscapes
that have marbled my neck

with dark
hairs   and sharp   coarse

longings.
    Ask me how I remember her –

not a face   but a movement

     legs stotting into a slip of boreal green.

A swatch of colour
     in the shape of a lost country.

A daughter   which is to say   an inherited
vanishing

     through the slit of a dream.

HOUSE OF PRAYER

I walk into the beads of thirty-three alhamdulillahs,
I walk into my childhood mouth, repeat *alhamdulillah.*

Four decades ago, father too walked into this prayer,
his body nested in the oblong Boeing, his alhamdulillah

humming deep until it matched the scale of the engine.
It was during that first crossing from one alhamdulillah

to another home, that my father crushed open the chasm
he has since passed down to every poem I write: [   ]

the hollow, the forgotten Qur'an lodged deep in the night
of an unopened drawer. My quest to belong. Alhamdulillah,

forgive me, forgive me. I praise once again, I symmetry
like the wings of a migrating bird, I repeat *alhamdulillah*

and rinse and repeat and rinse and repeat, like the *rokrok*
of an egret. I hold this tasbih to count my alhamdulillahs

thirty-three times, ninety-nine times: the key is to walk
again and again into the holy, repeating *alhamdulillah,*

alhamdulillah, alhamdullilah, until the skyward calm. Father,
what did you hope for when you uttered *alhamdulillah,*

when you whisked over the Atlantic in that giant bird?
When the egg cracked open and the yolk of alhamdullilah

spilled onto a new coast? Was it travelling homeward
or away from homeland? I have learned that alhamdulillah

does not resemble a border but is a house of its own.
Alhamdulillah glints beyond language: praise be to God.

My western tongue holds the syllables, unhooks the praise in
my own last name: h-m-d. Always, I recite *alhamdulillah*.

TASBIH

Walk into the turquoise bead thirty-
three times. This is a ritual like
rinsing the

darkdark

of your hair. The everglade birds
rokrok as they flicker in and out of the
wet. How thirsty are you, how holy?
In this flood, you will learn how to
make. Which is to say, you will nod
bend hinge drink and repeat. Listen:
the answer is in how the egret

rokroks

once more. To weave is to look inward
at each stage, then burgeon again.
Here you will learn how to symmetry,
how to pray, how to god.

BELIEF AS AN OCEAN LANDSCAPE

From you I was born
my body an isosceles triangle
with two equal sides
of longing:
what is given and what is prayed for
these pining lengths
yoked together by the latitude
of a risen country
I have never visited.
I imagine the view from the ocean
is your body and your body
is a tree struck down
because it is true
that we are portraits born
already holding the things we love
the barakat which
will unmake us.
When I was young I only knew
your nation of branches
every holy pinnacle
a wild deer to marvel at.
Now how the ocean
dips like a spine

embracing its hollows
revealing the Swahili coast
revealing how belief is also a plot
of land
on which we create
the ruminants we love.

ANOTHER LAST PRAYER

Bismillah   will you grant me the valleyed crevice of
something silver and scoured

with sound.
I wander toward guilt

a young traveller looking for ruins
loving what I can

jagged with the narrow edge of all I do not.

Prayer like bees in my mouth.

Allah like tasbihs   in my mouth.
How many times have I opened myself up to God?

The deer have returned from their rivering.

My tongue is sanded down by the language
of you   so what is left?

The wind, the wind, the wind
thirty-three times the bead flicks

like the *ki ki ki* of a northern bird

how it howls through my skin
into a landscape of wild hives –

What is left has no holy.

What is left is a nameless vine, frayed
and twinning into the moss.

Another prayer not unlike undoing the seam
of a wound to find a forest.

Every du'a a deep cut   every recitation its blood.

Again and again the wind.
Merciful Allah   grant me forgiveness if anything.

SELF-PORTRAIT AS A LOST LANGUAGE

We name our bodies / anything that means *to gather* / flock
& clique

into belonging / into the tamarack wood / into the mouths
of January

the month I buy a bag of sweet / seedless / plum tamarind
& leave

the fruit to rust / we stumble into our blood / wild animals
yoking together

an inheritance / this country of unrest / where loss is shade
beneath

every cracked tree / a frisson of terror / each time lightning
embosses

the fields / the circumpolar boreal / & commodious prairie
rippling

smaller on my tongue / we name our bodies / before they
are unnamed

by the grassland smoke / & the feckless eyes / of those who
mark us

with an *x* / this winter country / its season of amaranthine
oranges

& tender mangoes / I eat the pith & boil the rinds / I hope
the ghosts

of mother tongues / transpire in the vapour / I am drawn
to every scattering

syllable / stammerings of Kutchi / & coifs of clove to split
the sweet

of this memory / this version / an imagined Dar es Salaam
in a story

passed down / we collect the fragments / gather together
blanks

& birch / judge our own belonging / this dream is a basin
of other

dreams / longing slips through like words / my tongue is
a sieve.

ELEGY WITH TWO ELK AND A COMPASS

In Jasper, Alberta, I pass through the widowed poplars.
Evening hikes up her dark hems, trees begin howling their elegies,
when loosened from the thicket, two elk walk into my gaze.
Here, in the gap between needle point and destination
there is an unkind earth that persists even as loss petals down
leaving the poplars bare. Earlier that day, I crossed
the forest's bridges and stepped beyond its corridors.
I longed to find the hidden trail that led to the valley of roses.
From the elk I am expecting a lesson, as if Allah has approached me
in the shape of a compass built from antler and vine.
Their muscles tense. One rises into a gallop, widening the field.
Its legs seize with strength and I remain in the space left behind:
the sudden nakedness of a northern forest – I am unable to follow.
The elk, in their way, have mastered living by mastering letting go.

FIRE STARTER

This is the hum
of a northern forest.

Don't forget all of the salt
that has gone into this healing –

wince if you must,

call out to India for two hundred years
if you must.

I am building a home and
burning down

my body that has never felt
like my body,

drinking from a spring
to balance

all of this smoke.

I am building a fire
that snags

onto the redwoods.

I want to redesign this dish
my body was

born into,
glucose and brown skin

multiplying within the agar.
Hair that smells

like burning grass,
a landscape that reaches for

another land.

INVOCATION

Somewhere, they are kneeling
and I am forgetting your name,

how to hold each fragment
of sound in my mouth –

Allah,
my thoughts are scattering in the wind.

They land in Dar es Salaam,
in India,

in miles of golden grass.
Sometimes they fall into my own palms

as I pray next to my father
for my father.

My Father, I am discovering how
to feel loneliness

in a series of languages
by cutting open

each word like a sweet black plum
only to eat the skin.

Tell me I am a little closer
to the beginning

that I am a young tree on the side
of a mountain,

a recursive bird
gliding up a redwood,

or simply a sound travelling
vertical.

ON MY TONGUE

Bismillah is my first memory.

I became a bird in the Qur'an
at only eight years old.

I opened the dark green cover
and revealed the slippery

two hearts: Arabic
and its English translation.

On Saturdays, I learned to repeat
passages in Arabic,

to recite the Qur'an
in its truest language –

otherwise are the locusts
really locusts?

I read and read, yet
struggled to recite in Arabic.

This was not a problem
with my memory.

I learned in a week how
to recite the first verse in English.

Sometimes I think every Qur'an
has a dark green cover.

Sometimes I think I still
become a bird

when, in my mind, I remember
Bismillah, ar-Rahman, ar-Rahim.

This must be the reason I
continue to love.

On my tongue, there is
a short-horned grasshopper.

Bismillah, I reach for you again.

once, in childhood, a girl walked into her house of prayer
and became fog. the stories the great-greats pass down are
always about transformation: seed to pulp, saltwater to pearl.
somewhere, the deer are bounding into the snow, unaware of
each firing neuron, unaware of the river basin's rich soil. what
was the threshold of her muscle? how many fires were lit before
she leveed into ghost? in early january, they cross the grove in
groups of three, wet and for a moment, gliding. when the deer
land, something about the earth has changed. she crossed like
any other animal would. perhaps, too, licked at the frozen river,
kissed her reflection. it is unknown where she landed. once,
in childhood, her mother crossed water and split into so many
particles that at last, she became a discord of countless things: part
mule deer, part alluvial, part clear knowledge in the frozen wild.

AVIAN CIRCULATORY SYSTEM

Birds have proportionally larger hearts than humans.
With a heart the relative size

of a crow's to its body, I would need the blood of all my ancestors.

The problem isn't that I don't know my grandmother's first name,
or that I haven't shared the tartness of tamarind

with my mother on any Tanzanian island.

Physiologically, they are so alike: four-chambered, cone and crescent
shaped, but

the problem is night –
how daybreak transforms two identical stones into a motherland

and a daughter, depending on the snarl of grassland at their ankles.

I have spent too long wishing for the heart of something else,
bathing in a pond

in secret, so that I might hide the lacquer of my anatomy. I envy birds
that pump blood according to instinct,

never concerning themselves with the bloodline threading through.

ODE TO MY MOTHER'S HAIR

I hear Navroz and I picture roses every time.

A word the shape of things I cannot say

or cannot think to say. All the ways I am reminded
of you:

ache and root and chasm.

It is spring again and I am holding the watering can

        at your edge, willing

each of your nephrons to bud and flower anew.
It is spring again –

Navroz – meaning your hair, clipped now, will entrance

with its vivid warmth once more. Mother,

you are the silhouette of every spring I have gulped down.
It was such a long

winter, your body filled with dead seeds.

And all along, there was also this – every poem filled
with the shade of you,

even this ode to spring.

AFTERWARD

Lately, all we seem
to talk about

are the ghosts
that visit us as we dream.

I swear the moon
is halving itself as we speak

and everything else, too, is
lessening.

I rearrange the letters in *air*
until they become *loss*.

The light reaches us
more easily

through all of the dead trees.
I was a young girl

once, with dreams
of elk and hummingbirds,

with dreams
of my mother's hair

then, so full and black
and glistening.

I thought there must be suns
in every corner

of every room.
Where is anything now?

I look for anything
beyond the multiplied *hush*

of nine small pills
in the morning,

of mother's hair, black
strands

in the sink like loose
threads of silk.

Now, a deep echo
like the kind of emptiness

left behind once
all the birds have taken off.

All I can hear is
hush, hush, hush.

IN THE LEFTOVER SPACE

I picked the flower

and revealed the alternate world. I revealed all
the generations I'd once ushered from a garden pond.
The ghosts scattered like mice between the petioles,
sought more daylight than any ghost is allowed.
The flower receded to wherever displaced atoms go
in this homeland: a corpse planted back into the seed,
so far back into the seed that it became a window
framing all the women that came before. I picked
the flower and planted so far back into the seed.
Elsewhere, a daughter felt hands tug a strand of dark
hair into the varnished alternate world.

All the faces on the overlapping petals. Viola markings.
The wind, for example, still jostles the empty field.

ACKNOWLEDGEMENTS & NOTES

To my family, Mom, Dad, Reena, Shazna, and my partner, Tim, thank you for your care, for your support, for your fierce love. All of you are, in some way, within these pages.

All my love to Rebecca Ferrier, Jay Gao, Alyson Kissner, Nicole Lachat, Adi Onita, Pratyusha, Laura Schoenberg, and Jihyun Yun, whose friendship and support I cherish with my whole heart. I am so lucky that we are all on this beautiful journey of writing and creating together. I am forever grateful to my dear friends Nadine Aisha Jassat, Hannah Lavery, Amy LeBlanc, Jeda Pearl Lewis, Éadaoín Lynch, Alyssa Ogi, Andrés N. Ordorica, and Jayme Ringleb, who saw iterations of this manuscript, and whose continuous feedback was so necessary for this collection to take shape.

Thank you to the luminous poetry and fiction writers I studied with during my MFA at the University of Oregon. I would not be the poet I am today without our adventures together. I miss you all dearly and think about you often. And warmest of thanks to my teacher and thesis advisor, Garrett Hongo, whose encouragement gave me the confidence to pursue not only my creative writing, but also my PhD and academic research.

I am so, so grateful to my generous poetry teachers, Bert Almon, Danny Anderson, Geri Doran, Alan Gillis, Shawna Lemay, and Derek Walcott, and to my mentors, Eduardo C. Corral, Sarah Howe, Mimi Khalvati, and Sandeep Parmar.

Thank you for your continued generosity and advice. I will never be able to adequately express how much your guidance has meant to me, how much I continue to learn from the moments we spent together.

Thank you to the extraordinarily caring communities that invited me in with open arms: Scottish BPOC Writers Network and Ledbury Poetry Critics. And, to my brilliant PhD cohort at the University of Edinburgh, you will recognise many poems in this book. Thank you for so often being my first readers, and also my first friends in this wonderful city.

To everyone at East London Arts and Music, it was an honour to work with so many talented and kind young people and teachers. Thank you for celebrating my poetry with me during difficult times of isolation.

For me, writing poetry has always been about creating community. Thank you to everyone who has ever read and opened their hearts to my poetry. Publishing this collection has been a thrilling, terrifying, and ultimately beautiful act.

Thank you to my editors, KMA Sullivan (YesYes Books) and Edward Crossan (Polygon), for making this dream come true.

*

A heartfelt thank you to the editors, submission readers, and competition judges who first took a chance on my poetry. A special thanks to my mighty publishers ignitionpress and BOAAT Press for first publishing several of these poems in my chapbooks *Hinge* and *Faces That Fled the Wind*.

'Hinge' in *Gulf Coast: A Journal of Literature and Fine Arts*
'Love Poem with Elk and Punctuation', 'Prairie Storm', and 'Tasbih' in CBC Books
'House of Prayer' in *Palette Poetry*
'You Know It but It Don't Know You' in *Map Magazine* and shown at the Talbot Rice Gallery
'Self-Addressed' in *The London Magazine*
'The Fish That Halved Water' and 'Afterward' in *Arc Poetry Magazine*
'Hawwa Discovers Adam by the River' in *Third Coast Magazine*
'Avian Circulatory System' in *The Fiddlehead*
'Faded' and 'Endearments' in *Glass: A Journal of Poetry*
'Meditation While Plaiting My Hair' in *VIDA Review*
'I Want the Kind of Permanence in a Birdwatcher's Catalogue' in *SBWN Mixtape*
'After the House of Wisdom' in *Wasafiri*
'When the Wolves Appear' in *Tupelo Quarterly*
'Lapse' in *Poetry Wales*
'Midnight Vessel Across the Great Sea' in *Plume*
'Persephone's Crossings' in *Bedtime Stories for the End of the World*
'Elsewhere' and 'On My Tongue' in *The /temz/ Review*
'Origin of Water II' in *Southeast Review*
'Self-Portrait with Fish Eyes' in *Islands Are But Mountains*

'My Body Is a Forest' and 'Self-Portrait as a Lost Language' in
The Adroit Journal
'Fire Starter' and 'Invocation' in *Prarie Schooner*
'Another Way to Split Water' in *amberflora*
'Ode to My Mother's Hair' in *wildness*

A NOTE ON THE AUTHOR

ALYCIA PIRMOHAMED is a Canadian-born poet based in Scotland. She is the author of the pamphlets *Hinge* and *Faces that Fled the Wind*, and the collaborative essay *Second Memory*, which was co-authored with Pratyusha. She is the co-founder of the Scottish BPOC Writers Network, a co-organiser of the Ledbury Poetry Critics Program, and she currently teaches on the MSt. Creative Writing at the University of Cambridge. Alycia has held post-doctoral positions at the University of Edinburgh and at the University of Liverpool, and she received an MFA from the University of Oregon and a PhD from the University of Edinburgh. She is the recipient of numerous awards, including the 2019 CBC Poetry Prize and the 2020 Edwin Morgan Poetry Award.